Rabbits in Colonies

Boyd Craven Jr.

& A.Z. Nilsson

Introduction

Welcome to Volume 3 of The Urban Rabbit Project. This time we are going to focus on the possibilities of keeping Rabbits In Colonies. My name is Boyd Craven Jr. I'm going to tell you a story that shows you what I've been up to lately with my rabbits' living quarters. I'll show you some ideas that have inspired me and introduce my co-author for this volume, Zab Nilsson with whom you will be as thoroughly impressed as I am I promise. Then I'll give you an idea of where this seems to be taking me next! ☺

I was born in 1957. When I was a boy, my family lived in Grand Blanc, MI, USA in a very "country" setting. All around us were woods and fields, so I grew up appreciating wildlife. My father enjoyed hunting, and from probably 5 years of age, I followed him on his small game hunts. At 9 years, I got my first shotgun from Dad. I learned to hunt pheasant, cottontail rabbit and squirrel mostly. I didn't realize it until later that he was teaching me "how" these animals lived in the woods and in and around the farmer's fields and crops. By learning where and when to find them, I discovered their normal habits and food preferences. Pheasants were to be found around the edges of the farmer's corn and bean fields, near their preferred food. Squirrels live where the hardwoods met with corn fields eating nuts and corn. Rabbits however were to be found where thick tangles of wild raspberry brambles met thick brush and hay or winter-wheat fields. They liked to hide and hang out where most of their predators were uncomfortable or unable to go, and they liked to eat grass. Little did I know just how useful, in a different sort of way, these lessons would be to me later in my life.

As I grew up, so did the area where we lived. Farmers sold off building lots along the roadways to the ever increasing population in the area for houses. Apartment buildings, office buildings and shopping centers took more and more of the land. The farmer's land that he had so kindly allowed us to use for hunting, walking and learning about the wildlife was no more. There became fewer pheasants, as their habitat had disappeared and had been turned into grass lots for houses.

The 40-80 acre farms that were plentiful in my childhood are now mostly gone and the only real farming that has been going on for years is large, corporate farms. In just a few generations, people have lost the lessons my Dad taught me about wildlife. They don't have the pleasure of watching fields of food grow close at hand. They have lost touch with where their food comes from. The small to medium sized farms, with small to medium sized equipment, producing

4

small to medium sized crops of food have all been replaced with small lawn care equipment producing nothing but lawn refuse for the landfill. People get their "food" in neat little packages at the supermarket or worse yet from the drive through.

After too many years of being comfortable with this, too much obesity and too much sickness, we as a people are beginning to wake up and realize our mistakes. Local food, farmer's markets and growing garden vegetables are coming back in vogue. It wasn't until I retired at 48 years of age in 2006 that I regained my interest in gardening and raising rabbits as a meat section of that garden.

My family and I re-learned the modern day ways of raising rabbits together, but the lessons from a long time ago remained etched in my mind. This just seemed all a bit too clinical. There were too many "rules" and it was not sociable at all for the rabbits. Not the way I remembered animals living in the wild or even what I remembered from the farms. I was looking for a better way…

Table of Contents

Changing the Rules

The methods taught for raising rabbits these days have evolved just as much as the story I told above. Practically every book that I could find insisted that rabbits must be raised in an all wire cage, inside a building and fed nothing but commercial rabbit pellets. My mind knew that to be untrue, but to "prove it" to myself, then others we had to start with an accepted practice for where we live and EASE our way away from it, towards what I remembered, documenting in writing and with pictures as we went.

We started with all wire cages, but very high quality ones in our garage doing things exactly as is recommended these days. We fed only commercial pellets, clear water and some locally grown hay. We began with a trio of Californians, as recommended. Either we were lucky, or we followed directions well because we had very good success and a great deal of fun doing it. I'll not attempt to tell you that we made no mistakes or wasted no money while learning. We made every mistake I've ever heard of I think, and wasted enough cash to buy ourselves food from the grocer for a very long time, but we were determined to learn. As our herd grew and our knowledge grew, we began experimenting with every detail, all the while remembering and discussing what I had been taught so long ago. We didn't like keeping the rabbits in the garage. It wasn't bad in the winter as long as we kept the two 100 watt light bulbs burning all day to simulate daylight. In the summer, it got just entirely too hot in there for the rabbits to stay. I wasn't about to air condition the garage to raise a few rabbits in it! We HAD to change.

We changed their housing through a gradual evolution to wood and wire hutches that were weather tight that we kept outdoors in shady, protected places of the yard. We decided that our rabbits were much better off outdoors.

We included places for them to hide, relax and digest. We learned that if we made the spaces just the right size, the doe would build her nest in the dark back side of the hide when kindling, yet she still had enough room for herself just inside the doorway. That kept the kits where she wanted them as well as warming them with her body heat when needed just like a wild doe would do in her burrow. She will cover them more or remove some covering and store it right underneath where she's sitting depending on their immediate needs.

We made a removable floor in the hide/nest area that could just be taken out when it was time to "remove the nest box". This made huge improvements in our ability to keep their area clean. Clean, relaxed, well fed kits make healthy kits.

That hay rack on the right wall was a mistake. Those have all been removed. The kits learned that they could jump up there and it became their potty area of choice! Not easy to keep clean. Other than that, this setup has proved very successful for getting kits to the age of weaning. Just before they're old enough to wean, it starts getting just a bit crowded in the hutch, so something needed to be done.

To give mom a break, I took her litter outside the hutch in a wire cage on nice days in the shade of my red maple tree. This is a 24"x24". It's easy to carry and will hold a litter for me during the day from say 3 weeks old until 5 weeks old.

It worked in nice weather, but I couldn't leave them and all of us got wet quite a few times while I was running out to put them back in the hutch if it suddenly started raining. Also, there just didn't seem to be enough room for the rabbits to get as much exercise as I thought that they should have. Rabbits like to run, jump and chase each other.

This thought led me to build an exercise run large enough for them to really run, yet light enough for anyone to move. Below is the first model. Constructed out of 2"x3"s, it was 4' wide and 8' long. No bottom and no top. In the shade of that same red maple, I could put mom AND her litter out to exercise on nice days. I still couldn't leave them, as a big dog could jump right in and they'd be toast! I also found it difficult to round up the little guys and girls at bedtime to put them back in their hutch. So, we had to remodel! ☺

As you can see, they spent more time "grazing" than anything else. The little ones don't even try to get out. Before long we found ourselves calling this the "day grazer".

The next model was the same size. I used 1/2"x 1/2" hardware cloth on the sides. Raccoons cannot reach their hands through that and dogs cut their noses on the thinner wire if they attack it. I have witnessed both. It holds up.

The top was added to keep the buns in and predators out. Rather than make a hinged lid, this one is simply two pieces of 26"x8' corrugated PVC roofing over-lapped 2" in the middle and resting on cross braces. Notches are cut where wood framing is. They can be lifted right out, so that I or visiting children can climb right in.

I couldn't get him to pose for a better picture, but that is a mink on my dock after having no luck getting into the grazer to eat my rabbits.

There is still no bottom. I noticed right away that on really hot days, the buns in the grazer were much better off than those in wire cages 4" above the ground under the tree, or those in hutches in the shade. It was the contact with the ground that was helping to keep them cool.

An oblong plastic tub with no lid, bottom side up with an entrance hole cut in one end makes a good, lightweight place to hide in and maintain ground contact or to climb on top of. This allows flexibility, depending on how many rabbits I have in each grazer at a time. They're easy to wash and stack up compactly when not in use.

Those girls are climbing on and eating their way through a pile of freshly mowed grass that I just dumped into one corner. I dump it on the front end, in the direction I intend to move next, giving them more time with it and prolonging time between moves. After the grazer passes any remaining soiled grass gets raked up and scattered between rows in the garden. Ease and diversity of feeding forage is a definite advantage to this type of housing. The ground IS the feeder!

I use 20oz. water crocks resting on top of the bottom board. The smaller kits like to lay on the board too, sometimes in the sun, sometimes in the shade. They are free to choose.

My experience with this type of setup has been pleasant. I feel that the rabbits are happier and in better condition than caged rabbits, which for me, makes for better eating. My guests and neighbors enjoy watching the rabbits frolic and boats or passing kayakers will pause near the shore just to watch them.

Hopefully, you are getting a mental picture of the evolution of my rabbit husbandry practices here. I am slowly but surely headed towards a simpler, more natural rabbitat while not giving up the modern day advancements available to me.

Megan's Colony Hutch

Recently in my online travels following all things rabbit, I came upon pictures of an extremely clever, WAY different, yet really efficient type of rabbitat. It caught my eye. Megan Wilson has been developing a three story colony hutch for her rabbits with TONS of floor space, but a small footprint. I contacted her to interview her for this volume, and she was happy to share her experience with us.

Megan assured me that on this prototype she was going for functionality, not looks. Having "been there" myself, I understand where she's coming from. Pretty can come later!

Her colony hutch is 96 square feet. 8'x4'x3 levels high, with ramps connecting each of the levels. Each level is 2 feet tall to allow for standing and jumping. She plans to eventually add some shelves to the inside to increase floor space even more. She also has plans to create hiding places inside.

She says so far it's working very well. The rabbits spend about 90% of their time on the bottom floor together. The top two levels are only used occasionally. They seem to prefer to cuddle and groom each other than spend any real time alone, but the space is there and available if they choose. Holy cow, is it ever!

For her next addition, she added 3 new stacked single hutches on the left hand side of the colony. Those hutches are separated from the colony only by wire on the common wall. That gives the occupant the benefit of being "in" the colony, yet kept separate. Currently she has 3 bucks in those 3 hutches, but they are more than large enough to accommodate a doe and her kits or as a grow-out pen if needed. Each measures 4'x 3' or 12 square feet.

Here one can see the same ramp that was in the other picture, only now there is the whole new hutch beyond it completely open save the wire. It shares the warmth, allows for sociability and in this case allows Megan to control her breeding by keeping the bucks separate from the does.

I asked Megan some questions that came to mind, that I thought others might wonder as well. Here's what she said:

Q: What inspired you to try a colony setup?

A: I was inspired to do a colony set-up because of studies I had read showing rabbits were happier in colonies. In the wild, they will naturally live in a sort of colony set up, with a few females and one male in each territory. It was important to me that my rabbits be as happy and well cared for as I could possibly make them. I do have a few does that are not happy in a colony and will start fights, so I allow them to live separately. All the others are quite happy in a colony though, so they live together.

Q: What made you decide on the multi-story design?

A: I decided on a multi-story design for multiple reasons. Some of the more important reasons for me were that in a colony setting it is important to have many hiding places for the rabbits in case they need a break. Having a multi-level colony is kind of like having built in hiding spaces. They can go to a different floor to get away if needed (although it's very rare, for the most part they all choose to stay together on the same floor).

The other reason is that I'm short on yard space. I wanted to give the rabbits as much square footage as possible without reducing my yard space. If you can't build out - build up!

Q: What have you discovered about a multi-story colony that is good/convenient vs. bad/inconvenient?

A: The convenient part of colony raising is that it's a lot less work. All of the rabbits use the same potty corner. They share feed stations and water stations. They entertain each other so I don't have issues with rabbits chewing on the cages or always trying to escape. They're so happy in the colony with their buddies that they have no reason to want to leave. My individual rabbits are much higher maintenance.

The inconvenient part is that the cage is very large and deep, so it can be an issue to catch the rabbits. Since I only breed once or twice a month, I don't really find it a huge deal. If I needed to catch all of the rabbits every day it would be much more of an inconvenience, but that's not really a huge issue for me. There are ways to deal with that, like building a trap door near the feeders, or having a cage that's more shallow. Because it doesn't bother me much I haven't set that up.

Q: Would you recommend a colony to a "brand new" Rabbiteer?

A: I would absolutely recommend colonies to a brand new rabbit person. Seeing your rabbits running and playing and getting to live happy lives is very rewarding. I think happier rabbits=lower stress=healthier meat.

Q: What would you do different next time?

A: If I were to re-build my colony cage I think I would do pretty much the same thing, but I would make it prettier. It's built out of just basic plywood, and has a tarp on top to keep the rain out. Not very attractive! It was only my prototype, next time I'll use some nice wood, maybe paint the outside, and give it a slanted roof with shingles to keep the rain out instead of an ugly blue tarp.

Q: Are you planning for more?

A: Right now I'm quite happy with the colony I have. It functions very efficiently. I'm not planning to add any more breeders to my set-up. In the future I may build a more attractive version of the same thing.

Notes:

I am really impressed with this concept. With what Megan has going on, I could immediately see how I could incorporate all of the things I like about my hutches and grazers that I just told you about into one place while adding tons of space. A colony hutch sounds like it will save me tons of work too. It wouldn't be moveable like my grazers, but there are always ways to work around that. This definitely gives me ideas! You can meet Megan Wilson in the Rabbits in Colonies group on Facebook.

Before going any further, I want to introduce my co-author for this volume, and turn it over to her for a while.

Zab Nilsson

Zab is from Sweden. She lives halfway around the planet from me, is from a totally different generation than me, but we share an interest in natural living conditions for our rabbits. Besides being a very talented graphic artist, she has the absolute coolest fixed colony I've seen. She's WAY ahead of me on this one and I'm very proud of her! She has agreed to tell us all about it here.

Owner: **Rabbits in Colonies**
www.facebook.com/groups/371075886338611/

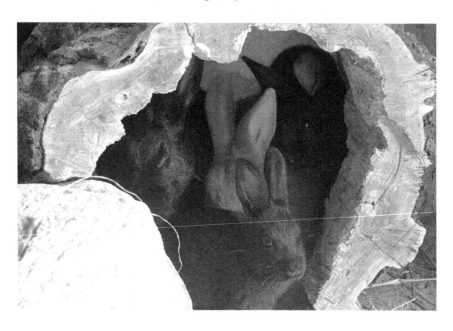

I got my first rabbit 13 years ago. He was a pet, a wonderful mini-lop cross named Zplit. I've had numerous different animals in my life, including him and several other rabbits those 3 years before I went to boarding school and decided they needed more attention than I could give, but Zplit was special and one of the pets I'll always remember.

We competed in rabbit jumping and won quite a few contests at the time. We even became club champions one year, my little cross and me. What I really loved was how I could take him on walks, unleash him and be sure that once he had taken a run around the area he'd look back to make sure I followed him, or he would come back and stand on his hind legs to make me pick him up. He showed me what a great pet rabbits can be. That is one of the things that made it obvious to me that it's simply not right to keep a rabbit in a small hutch their entire life. They are not teddy bears, but living creatures with energy and needs to move about. They are actually quite clever animals, and they don't get less clever just because we have them for meat.

I did keep Zplit in a regular Swedish, home built outdoor hutch that my dad built for me. I think the largest we had was a 1m x 1m. I kept my other rabbits the same way. At that time I took my rabbits out on walks in a leash, and I also had a playpen where they got to exercise themselves. With Zplit, I just set him loose in the garden. Back then I had rabbits for pets. I had two different types of hutches. The first ones were single hutches, standing on legs, with a fully enclosed part and an outside part. The bottoms were solid (I'll talk about that later) and they had access from the top.

Except that I used chicken wire and often found Zplit hopping about in the garden, they worked well. The top loaded part made them a bit difficult to clean, but with only a couple of cages it was no problem.

As I expanded, my loving father built me more cages. We built one in three levels, standing like a tower and the bottom floor was just inches above the ground. It was one meter by one meter and all three floors had removable houses. I think we used better wire by then. I don't have any photos that show it well, but I will add one picture and draw another to show. In the traditional Swedish hutch a nesting spot is usually integrated and sometimes a hayrack. Usually both the house and the play area have doors. As I don't have any photos of my own from this type of hutch, but still think they're worth mentioning, I've painted one.

Those cages opened from the front, and the large opening made it easy to reach and to simply rake out any bedding. Usually they're built in two or three levels with two rows, making it a four or six hole hutch.

Now, when I got new rabbits after a decade without, my purpose was different. I don't intend to show jump with them or keep them as pets, but I keep them for meat. Knowing that they are the thinking and needing creatures they are, even if I won't spend much time with them I realized that I can't keep them in cages never to get out and move, and still feel proud of myself. I do not mean to judge anyone who does keep their rabbits caged, I am well aware that it is a very common and accepted way to keep rabbits both for pets, meat or show. Still, it's not the way I find fair.

So how should I go about it, then? I wanted meat rabbits because I disagree with the meat industry's way of keeping animals, but I still believe that human beings have the same right to eat meat as other carnivores or omnivores. I want my rabbits to be able to move about and have a social life for the time they do live. A colony seemed to be the way to go. I figured it would be easier than to keep them in separate, huge cages. I thought also that they would enjoy each other's company. I've had meat rabbits only since December 2012, but I've still had the time to make mistakes, change my mind and learn a thing or two. These are the experiences I want to share with you now.

Why a Colony?

I've mentioned this before, but I'll say it again. I believe a colony setting to be the best option for housing rabbits, if it's properly set up. I also think that a colony is a very easy way to keep rabbits. There's only one pen to clean and put food and water in, instead of several smaller hutches. In Sweden, we have a few laws on how to keep rabbits. One is that they are not allowed to stand on wire mesh floors. This means that hutches need a solid floor and bedding material to soak up urine and bunny berries. If you have five hutches with rabbits, that means five potty-corners. In most cases you'll need to clean out each hutch's bedding entirely. In a colony, you usually get a few potty-corners. Mine has two. In a colony like mine you have room to stand and room to move around, which makes cleaning it easier still. I find it possible to keep a deep layer of bedding to which I add straw or other bedding material from time to time. Then, once every few months I empty out the entire colony. This can be done in a hutch, but it's more troublesome and will decrease the rabbits space since the floor will rise between cleanouts. I have decided for a more regular clean-out once a week, more about that later.

Why do we have this non-wire law, then? It's an animal welfare law. My first thought of it is because wire is rough on their paws, whether they actually get sore or not. This is what we assume over here anyway, although I have started to doubt that one part. Another, but to me very valid reason is that a wire floor is quite boring.

We also have a law that requires rabbits to have nesting material, or "braid-able material" in their cages. This usually means straw or hay and the reason is that it gives the rabbits an outlet for their basic needs to dig and burrow, and to nest. This law is the same for bucks and does alike since the both sexes have this instinctive need to scratch and entertain themselves even if only does usually make nests. I have seen the occasional buck making nests and even pulling fur, but I would assume this to be abnormal behavior from a buck.

Swedish law requires hay or other forage feed on a free choice basis as well. Rabbits are meant to graze and eat most of the day. They need the fiber and to chew most of the day. Hay is simply the closest thing we can easily get to provide them with healthy natural fiber in their diet. Pellets won't fill that function even though they are a great additional feed to keep the rabbit's weight and help meet the rabbit's nutritional needs. Another law we have here is that the rabbit must have a house and a shelf in the hutch. The roof of the house can be used as the shelf. In a colony setting, all rabbits must have enough space to sit on the shelf or in the house(s) at the same time.

I personally think that these laws are great and I definitely see the point behind them. However I don't think this is enough for a rabbit who will spend its entire life in that hutch. In a colony, I can provide them with all of the above, as well as give them the possibility of social interaction as well as more room for them to move about. I believe that five rabbits sharing an area of 2 by 5 meters in a colony have more room to move about than five rabbits in a 2 by 1 meter hutch each. It's also easier to provide a fun playground for them without interfering with the potty-corners and making it hard to clean the pen, if they share the larger area. I love watching them interact with each other. It's like having a really neat fish tank, only better!

So, what are the dangers with a colony?

The first and more difficult danger is of course if you get rabbits that simply seem to hate each other. Getting a group of rabbits that function well together can be tricky, but there are some things to think about that can make a difference.

One is to have enough of food and water. Rabbits, like most animals, get territorial when they're hungry. I make sure to have several feed stations, especially for hay. A few different water stations help as well. I stay and watch so I know that all rabbits can get to the feed.

Give them several hiding spots and shelves, and enough room. It's all about removing the reasons to fight over things they need.

Another idea is to make sure that no single rabbit can see all of the pen at any given time. This can be arranged by making a hill, a clutter of bushes or adding logs and stones and tunnels in the center of the pen. Make sure some spots or parts are hidden even if a rabbit stands on the pile of logs in the center. The reason for this is that for one it makes the pen "feel" larger for them, but maybe more importantly: If a rabbit see all the other rabbits all of the times, she will keep track on them and have them on her mind. If they disappear out of view they won't be annoying her for the moment. And the low rank rabbit won't have to hide in a hole all the time but can simply make sure to hop around on the other side of the pen than the dominant doe. It's still important to avoid hiding spots where they get trapped, as that can call for pretty nasty fights and even injuries when they can't get away. I don't always keep this rule in my own rabbitats, and if you keep a pair and they go along very well it may not be necessary, but it's nice.

If possible, it's better to introduce a couple or few new rabbits at once rather than throwing a single rabbit in with the ones already living in the colony.

Be careful of introducing a lop eared rabbit to a colony of rabbits with standing ears, or the other way around. I have heard and experienced that lops can get issues with the others. Perhaps it is because the communication suffers from the dropped ears and that the lops can't receive or give warnings very easily to the others. I had a lovely white and grey lop in my original colony. She was very gentle and sweet but after a while I noticed tufts of white hairs in the colony. She often sat alone and soon enough I found bite marks and wounds. I removed her from my colony and she ended up with a friend. She was a very friendly doe. My other does are usually friendly to each other. Even when they are acting cranky, they just charge at whichever rabbit they dislike, but they never bite or keep a chase going. I have not found one bite mark since the lop was removed. Now, I'm not saying that it's impossible to keep lops and other rabbits together, I do know of a few success stories. However, this may be something to think about when you decide on your first rabbits.

Another thing to remember is to give them a chance to find out their "pecking order". Expect chasing and perhaps even some tufts of hair flying in the beginning. You may want to interfere if they draw blood, if a rabbit gets cornered and can't move away or if the chasing keeps going on for too long, but the bottom line is to allow them to sort things out. Avoid getting hysterical or interfering too much, just keep a watchful eye to avoid injuries.

When you have introduced your rabbits and things start to cool down after a day or two, take a good look on them. Try to see which is the most dominant and who is the least. See if everyone gets to feed and water and if someone is sitting alone most of the time. Check them for injuries or weight loss. You will have to touch and feel for both of those. The lonely rabbit may be picked on by the others and lead a very stressful life in the colony, even if it appears calm and friendly. The answer may be to add another doe or remove the loner.

How big should it be?

I often see questions on how big do you need the colony to be? To be honest, I don't have any set rules. A first idea might be to see what the minimal area a rabbit kept in a group requires by the law where you live, if there is such a law. Currently in Sweden that area is 0.35m2 for my size of rabbit. Now I think that's too small and I doubt I'd be able to keep the rabbits from fighting if I used that size for standard, but it is good to know things like that before you build. I think a pen of 12 by 12 feet may be good for three or four does without a buck. I would say that bigger is better, if you can give them more space then do so, but this is the recommendations I follow. My colony was originally a little larger to start with and not perfectly square. I have divided it into two pens with less does in each now.

As for height, that is something to consider as well. A tall fence may be more expensive and seem unnecessary considering the size of the rabbits, but it makes a world of difference for you when you're cleaning and working in the pen. In my outdoor pens, or grow-out pens, I need to keep my head down. If I use tools - like shovels or rakes - they tend to hit the roof while I work and that is highly annoying. I also wish I had made the grow-out pens larger from the start. So don't be cheap on size and space, you want it to be good from start.

Another thing you definitely need to consider is where to place the colony. A colony is usually more difficult to move around than a hutch, unless you build it in the shape of a rabbit tractor.

You want the colony to be protected from the weather. Rabbits suffer from warmth, winds and rain. If you're building the colony indoors, let's say in a barn, you won't have to think about this. But outdoors you'll be wise to put a roof on at least most of the colony, and some sort of walls around it to keep winds out. It's not always necessary to cover the sides from floor to roof, it can actually be nice to leave some part of the top on the wall open (with a net of course) to increase ventilation, especially in warm weather. If you live in a warm climate, the walls will provide shade. Having three walls and a roof is a good rule of thumb.

Perhaps you'll place the colony in a very protected spot in your garden, and thus only need a roof. However you make it, the rabbits need shade on sunny days, to be protected from rain and to be shielded from wind. And yet, they need light. You might want to provide artificial light for them if they live in a barn. Without light they may have trouble reproducing.

Rabbits generally withstand cold very well, but a box filled with straw will certainly help as they can burrow in there and the straw insulates and keep their body heat with them.

My Colony and Predators

When I made my colony I used a horse stall. I put up a net around it that was less than 1x1 inch mesh and two meters tall. On top of it I had a very thin plastic net. It discouraged my barn cats from jumping into the colony. I eventually got my first litter of kits and everything seemed to work out just fine. The kits became four weeks old and I started to feel that my colony was indeed safe enough. They spent more and more time outside the nest and one day two of the ten kits were gone and a third one was bitten across the shoulder. I couldn't imagine any of my does biting a kit that age and I started to fear that the rats had found their way in. Every barn and town have rats, even if they're good at hiding sometimes. I went over the colony and secured a few spots I figured may have been the entrance. A couple of days later I found another kit missing. I changed the roof for a better net, believing that must be their way in. The stress of having people building and fencing in the colony caused one kit to get sick and die from a twist in the intestines. With the roof changed I started to feel safe. Then almost a week later, another kit was lost. I found that one half eaten in a hole we had tried to cover up once already. The back of the colony is wood and stone and the rats had chewed through the wood. After that incident I've put several layers of concrete and net over the stone, floor and wall, as well as screwing metal around the bottom of the whole colony (which was wood only). It has now been some months without further losses and I can only hope my effort is enough. Learn from my mistake and make sure your colony is safe from rats as well as other predators. Rats and weasels will climb high up and squeeze through any hole they find, or chew if they're motivated enough. So don't let them find out about the tasty kits you keep in your colony or they'll be harder to keep out than they were from the start.

My colony with wire mesh roof and metal around the wood near the floor. Later the door also got a metal cover at the bottom.

My grow-out pens. One side for bucks, one for does. Note the ventilation part above the walls. I have since this picture built another one behind it, to use as well.

Getting Started Yet?

So, you now have your colony pen. Let's say it's 12' by 12' and you intend to keep three or four does in it. The bottom is either concrete or soil with a net dug down to keep the rabbits from digging out or predators to dig in. It has a safe roof and a nice, big door for you to get in without problems as you balance a water bucket in one hand and a bunch of hay pinned down under your other arm while you close the door. It's placed where it has shade and light and good air. Now what?

Now it's time for the fun part! To designing the rabbits home and add things for them on which you can enjoy watching the younglings hop around. The first item on the list is shelves. Put as many and big shelves you can without making it difficult to reach under them. The shelves provide more floor space for the rabbits as well as hiding spots beneath them. Make sure any shelf or ramp has a good footing and is not too high, up. I wouldn't put a shelf higher than 90cm from the floor unless it had something there to keep the rabbit from jumping down. Make ramps and ways on and off the shelves on both ends, or else one rabbit can block the ramp and keep another rabbit cornered. You don't necessarily need a ramp. A stair made with objects or lower shelves works just as well. You'd be surprised to see how high those three week old kits can jump on their own!

I mentioned distractions, this is an idea to try to enrich their habitat as well as block their view of each other. An idea for a toy or enrichment: Take a board and make sure it's broad and steady, preferably thick and somewhat heavy. I screwed three boards together to give it a better base. Drill holes in the board, in the center so it won't tip over so easily. Then stick branches in the holes. It's fun for the rabbits to stand up and reach and gnaw on it, and it's fun for you to watch.

Then you want nesting boxes if you are going to breed. Rabbits will use the spot they like best to nest in, and they want to have their own private "hole" so just make lots of hiding spots and make sure they can be used for nesting as well. Examples can be hollowed logs or handmade wood hutches. It can be a low shelf with wooden walls below it which separates it into different holes. Or it can just be whatever boxes, tubes or things you have at hand. It's always a good thing if they can be both on top of it and hiding under it.

Tunnels… rabbits love tunnels. If you can, provide it. They may choose to nest in a tunnel though, or be difficult to catch. Making one you can open or making them fairly short can be a good idea.

This is my old nesting box with the roof off. It has a tunnel as well and both will work as shelves when the lids are on.

I personally love nature-inspired things in my colony. I have hollowed logs that my father found, and I have a few rocks ad branches as well. The one wall in my colony has a stone-base, which I've filled with concrete. the rabbits often run up on the side or rest on a stone that's not completely covered with the concrete. But I also had nesting tunnels which I made from old floorboards. I write "had" because I've made new ones now which however has the same function but is made with a different wood. They have lids on them and also work as a stand for me so I can reach comfortably into the buck's cage. They are not very pretty and their square form is far from natural but they are functional.

Below you can see one of my new nest boxes. It's made with a removable roof but with different boards and a somewhat different design.

Bedding

You'll need some sort of bedding in the colony, unless you make a hanging all-wire colony pen. I'll list the types of bedding I have any experience with.

Straw is a simple and easy choice.

Bunny berries will fall through the top layer, leaving it fresh looking and dry. The rabbits will choose potty corners no matter what bedding you use, and in these it will be easy to just put new, fresh straw on top. You can change the straw often, or just keep adding new and change it every few months. When I clean the potty corners (or when I cover them to keep them fresh between cleanings) I use the fresh straw from the area around it to fill it up. I add new straw to the middle, that way I'll have a good circulation of the straw, not leaving any part of it in the colony for too long, and also not wasting any of it by throwing it out before it's actually "used".

The bed will start composting in the bottom while the middle and top layer creates a seal which keeps odor down if you decide to just add new bedding on top and clean all of it out every few months, which is another option. This may seem unsanitary but it is a natural process and if it is kept properly the rabbits will stay clean and healthy. If it smells or look bad, you need more straw or you have digging rabbits, either way the bedding is not kept properly. The composting process will create some warmth for the rabbits so this is a great option if you live in a cold area. The whole bedding will provide a nice footing for the rabbits as well. The downside is that if the rabbits like to dig in the wrong spot, they'll dig up the compost and the seal will be broken. For some reason I have never experienced or known anyone to experience this problem though. Another issue may be that the rabbits can hide a nest very well in the straw, and you may not find the kits until they climb out at three weeks old. It does take up a lot of space as I remove it, compared to shavings or peat. I need to get the wheelbarrow into the colony every time I clean. With other bedding materials it's usually enough with a bucket and small hand shovel.

Shavings are popular bedding.

While it will soak the urine and looks very light and fresh when it's new, I have found that every single bunny berry will be visible and impossible to hide, which makes it look unclean very fast and forces you to change a lot of bedding that is still fresh and nice, because it is mixed with the little black dots. I use shavings in the bottom of the potty corners and in my outdoor colony. I have heard of people using sawdust and sifting the bedding like I did with sand. In the outdoor colonies I prefer shavings because it won't be soggy like straw or peat gets and stays easy to clean even when wet, in difference to sand. If you have sand, you may not need a lot of bedding in an outdoor colony.

Sand is one option.

It can be sifted and re-used. As long as it is dry, it is easy to sift on the spot, removing the rabbit feces and leaving fresh sand. I did this almost every day on the parts of my colony where I had sand. After a while, I noticed a faint smell as I sift it, this means that the sand has been contaminated, perhaps with urine, and then I'll shovel it up, wash it in a bucket of water and let it dry in the sun.

Sand will be warm in sunny spots and cold in shaded parts, allowing the rabbits to use the best spot at the time being. If it's too deep it can put stress on the tendons in their feet but the right depth will be good for them. My rabbits seem to love rolling and scratching in the sand. It can be too hard and solid on their feet if it's not deep enough, at least if you have a wood or concrete floor and eventually I got tired of sifting every other day so I decided to change back to straw.

Peat is a material I liked a lot to start with.

It was very absorbent and even a very thin layer (half an inch to an inch) felt soft and springy to the touch. The downside is that it makes the ground pretty dark and it's fairly expensive. The price of it made me turn back to straw yet again, at first I noticed it lasted longer as I only needed a thin layer and it's so absorbent. Two of my does pee like horses though, so I considered mixing peat with shavings in their potty corner, to save a few pennies. Another good thing with peat is that the low Ph of it makes bacteria and fungus unhappy, and that's always good. It's easy to clean, looks neat and tidy and keeps smell down.

However as I used it for a while it got dry, and the springy, soft feeling disappeared which meant I would need a lot more to keep my rabbits feet happy. Because of that I turned back to using shavings and straw, it would get too expensive. It's also good to note that peat may be a bad choice for the environment. Here in Sweden we have a lot of it and it's not harming our nature to use it. This I asked a friend, who works with deciding if an area or piece of nature should be protected or not, so I trust her on that. While in other places it may be like cutting down rainforests and really disturb the natural balance. It also has an effect on the soil where you dispose of it.

Newspaper. There are cut newspapers to buy. I expect it to be a bit like shavings but less dusty. You could of course put old newspapers in the whole colony, or just in the potty corners, but it makes for a fairly hard surface, and is not overly absorbent. I know of people using it in indoor cages and I suppose it works well in a smaller cage where you can put a lot of it down. The print is supposed to help with sores, and yes you can get sore hocks even on a solid floor if it's too hard rather than springy. Especially if you don't keep the nails properly trimmed, I'm afraid I've made that mistake.

Putting a newspaper down in the colony once in a while makes for a good toy as well, many rabbits like to shred it.

The ink is somewhat toxic though, but I have yet to learn of a rabbit actually getting sick from it.

Mixing bedding

It is of course possible to mix beddings. I have had sand in one part of my colony, where the nesting boxes and hollowed logs were. The potty corners were covered with straw since I find the constant washing of wet sand to be bothersome, and one side of the colony had a stripe of straw next to the wall. It's a spot between two potty corners and I rarely stepped there, so I wasn't worried about accidentally stepping on a hidden nest. The rabbits can burrow and mess with the straw as well. If you use straw as a man bedding, some shavings in the bottom of the potty corners are great to absorb the urine and keeping it from leaking out outside the colony or into the rest of the pen.

When it comes to houses or hutches I want to have them filled to the breaking point with straw, especially outdoors. It insulates both against cold and warmth and rabbits are nesting and digging creatures.

I currently use straw, it's winter, I have access to it and I like it. Of the materials listed above, straw and shavings are what I keep coming back to.

Hopping into a cozy, straw-stuffed house is a real treat in the winter.

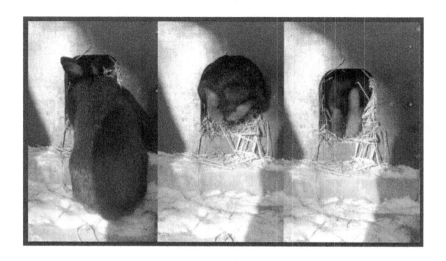

Related things

I have also started to use a product called Stalosan F, I've learned it's supposed to be available outside Sweden too and if not there should be some similar product to use. Stalosan is a non-toxic powder consisting of iron, copper and phosphates for the most part. It's used to prevent coccidia and insects by making the environment unfriendly for them and their eggs while still being perfectly safe for the rabbits. I have before mostly used Stalosan in stables with horses, as it prevents ammonia smell and flies. I have a friend who's horse loved to lick on the Stalosan, so much the owners got worried. It searched until it found it under the bedding, but it never got sick or unwell from it and that is something that ensures me of the products safety. I should note that this far, none of my rabbits have been interested in tasting it.

I just put some of the powder over the potty corners before I put fresh bedding on, about once a week. It has kept the amount of flies down, before I started with it I noticed some flies starting to creep out from the potty corners, but that stopped again with this wonderful pink powder.

Another option is to use limestone, I have no experience with it but it's supposed to have similar properties.

Sanitizing and coccidiosis

No matter how well you care for your rabbits, there's a chance that they will get sick or diseased for some reason. Coccidiosis is a common parasite that's hard to get rid of as it's very durable - it can survive for more than a year in the ground as oocytes.

Coccidia is a one-cell parasite that needs to be eaten by the rabbit in order to reproduce. While rabbits can have it in wire bottom cages - they eat their soft fecal droppings straight from the source - the risk gets greater when they have access to their feces like they do on solid bottoms.

I believe in the "get rid of it once and for all" approach which means that I will treat the rabbits with an effective medicine to kill the parasites in the rabbit, and proceed to kill the parasite in the cages.

I will issue a warning against using preventative drugs. It's called resistance and opposite to some peoples believes it's not the rabbit, horse, cat or dog that gets resistant, it's the parasite or bacteria. We have some types of worms and bacteria that is already resistant to most modern medicine. The problem with this is of course that we can't cure people or pets from it any longer. This in turn means that you can scrub your knee or get a cold and actually die from it. It also means that common surgery increase the chance of death of the patient. Every year in the United States, about 23 000 people die due to infections of resistant bacteria (according to Centers for Disease Control and Prevention). And that number is increasing as more bacteria get resistant against more antibiotics. In Europe it's currently 25 000 people (European Commission). Antibiotics have only been around for some 70 years but we are already dependent on them. Some surgical procedures cannot be performed at all without it. Remember this next time you consider to put a dab of antibiotic paste on a wound just for good measure.

The cause of the resistance is excessive use of drugs, not going through with a started treatment (if you stop when symptoms stop there may be weakened bacteria left that in turn adapts and gets resistant) and regular, low dose use of the drugs. Even with a forceful, complete treatment, parts of the drug will get through the rabbit and out into the nature where bacteria may adapt to it. The meat and food industry is to blame for some part as it's not uncommon to feed daily doses of drugs in preventative measures, but that doesn't mean that the rest of us can ignore the problem that's arising. Make sure to read the label on your rabbit feed as well as some feeds contain antibiotics and probiotics. Probiotics may not cause resistance, but it will help both the good bacteria and the bad, and it may actually mess up the rabbit's digestive system as that functions with the help of bacteria. This is also why some antibiotics can cause real harm and death to a rabbit, if you use the wrong kind.

This is **IMPORTANT**!

Do not use antibiotic ointments, daily wormers or the likes, it's causing long term, real problems. If your rabbit gets an injury, try iodine, salt or just clean water first. Creamy ointments in thin layers or honey are other examples of how to treat wounds.

Don't use the antibiotic creams or give antibiotics "just in case". Rabbits, just like cats, have great healing capabilities. It's amazing how well they heal even quite large injuries.

I'll just post this as an example - in Sweden you can't buy any antibiotics at all without a prescription. We treat with water or possibly iodine or alcohol (rarely alcohol as it stings). I don't know of a single case where an animal got a cut that was treated this way, and died of a general infection. Of course if they lose general condition and the wound gets over infected, we take them to the vet for a proper treatment, possibly with antibiotics. But that rarely happens. So please for the sake of world health, do NOT use drugs for preventative reasons, especially not antibiotics.

Same goes for dewormers. If you see any sign of worms then of course treat, but not by routine. If you feel insecure or just want to make sure you're not missing a case of worms, take a fecal sample and send it for analysis. Many people have started doing this and most find out that the cost of the analysis is paid multiple times by the saved money from not buying unnecessary drugs.

As for "alternative" treatments, such as yoghurt, pumpkin seeds, garlic, honey and whatnot, they may have an effect. Some may have a nutrient or substance that naturally deters some parasite or bacteria. I don't know enough about them to say which, but where there is a substance, there is a risk of resistance. As for garlic, there are reports in horses showing that excessive use over time lead to anemia and other problems. Horses and rabbits are not all too different in digestive matters, so I would handle garlic with care. Other 'natural' treatments don't affect the disease or parasite at all, but they boost the immune system and helps by providing nutrition for the rabbit. This is of course alright and won't cause resistance. Although it will not kill the parasite - if we talk about parasites - it will, in the best scenario reduce it or make the rabbit less susceptible. The best approach is however a preventative approach. Just be aware that probiotics and prebiotics may upset the rabbit's natural intestinal bacteria, and sometimes probiotics also helps the wrong bacteria to prosper in the rabbit.

Anyhow, back to the coccidiosis. Let's say you've found it in your herd and you got the right drugs to treat them. Then you need to treat the cage, but you realize that there are certain risks with torching wooden cages or pens. Perhaps like me you have the pen in a 200 years old, dry barn full of straw and hay close to the rabbits pen. Bleach doesn't kill coccidiosis, neither does Virkon S or other common disinfectants. Ammonia does, however. And heat, coccidiosis die at 55-60°C so torching is a good method where it's possible to do. Warm water with Natrium Hydroxide will also kill coccidiosis as it dissolves the proteins and lipids they're constructed by. It will burn and damage your skin and may cause blindness if you get it in your eyes - make sure to protect yourself with rubber gloves, perhaps a raincoat and pants and of course shield your eyes and preferably your entire face. It can develop a lethal gas in contact with aluminum so be careful with that. It can discolor the wood and damage paint jobs. Just as a side note, it's also used to make soap, glaze pretzels and can olives. But if you decide to use it to sanitize a pen, scrub the area clean, make sure the solution reaches everywhere and let it sit an hour or so. Then rinse really, really well. Once it's mixed up with enough water it's not bad for the environment or critters. It's the strong concentration that makes it effective.

I did this with my pens, and I boiled the bowls, crocks and

hay feeders, torched the wire and pretty much everything I dared to torch. I made floors for them to be able to sanitize as dirt is near impossible while wood is fairly easy.

At first I bought a Steam Cleaner. I found one that was cheap and simple, for dirty works. My reasoning is that a steam cleaner should reach about 130°C, which is good for coccidiosis that dies at 60°C as well as most bacteria. It doesn't burn down your barn and you don't need to inhale chemicals. 130°C was the temperature we used in the autoclave for sterilizing surgery equipment when I studied. However when I tried it, it didn't cover much of the area and I wasn't satisfied with the heat at all. So I decided not to use it further. I used the natrium hydroxide method instead.

For bacteria you may want to use other disinfectants as well or instead. Pasteurella dies within a day or two, so if that's the concern you can just clean the cage and leave it for a while. Disinfecting with heat or the like is not wrong, of course.

Now dirt floors and grounds is a problem especially with coccidiosis in mind. You can torch it, turn the soil and torch it again, unless there's a net in the way. It may or may not be enough. Be aware of grass roots that may start to burn and spread a fire quite far underground. Or you can leave the pens unused for a couple of years.

I have decided to use wooden and concrete floors only as they are possible to disinfect properly.

The Buck and a Rabbit Tractor

How to keep the buck then? I keep my does separated from my buck. This is because I want to keep control on when they breed and know when I may expect kits. I don't want the does to be bred back immediately after kindling and the kits weaned too soon. I keep my buck, Koriander, in a cage I've mounted on the wall in the colony. It's a large, solid bottomed cage (3.4 by 8.4 feet). Since it's on the wall it doesn't interfere with the space the does have. From this cage he can see the does, and it's easy to place a doe in his cage for breeding. I can open the entire front if I need to, because with a large cage like that you need big doors to access all of it.

I built it by making a frame for the floor to rest on. This was secured onto the wall and then we put a floor on top of it. Now you don't have to use hardwood oak floor boards, we just happened to have that at hand. It's actually quite slippery, so it's not the best option.

With the floor on top I also covered the walls with the same wood to protect them. I then built a frame for the wire. Then to make it easy to build I just put up some wire walls made for composting bins. They're cheap to buy and can be used as doors without making more frames or such.

Showing the placement of his cage as well as the frame it's resting on. You can just put a table into the colony and place a cage on that, if you want it easy.

While writing this text I have also built myself a rabbit tractor, inspired by Boyd's grow-out set up. My first intent was to keep the rabbits on a rotating schedule in it, so all of them got a few hours to graze. The bucklings until noon, then the doelings and the next say perhaps my breeding does. When it was the bucklings turn however, I noticed their first fight. It lasted just a few minutes but it was intense, a chase and even some actual fight with two of them lying down and kicking each other. Then it was all peace and quiet again but I got worried.

I searched around for answers and the most sensible one was that by being moved to a new territory, they needed to decide a new pecking order. Since I don't want to trigger them into a fight as I hope they can live together untill 6 or 7 months of age, I decided not to let them graze. I bring them fresh forage instead. My grazing cage is not big enough to house them permanently.

As it turned out however, I got a good use of the grazing pen as I turned it into a permanent cage for a spare buck. I bought a couple of new rabbits and one of them was a buck I hope to breed, but that meant I needed a new cage and the tractor was perfect for that considering I didn't use it much after the bucklings fight. It turned out to be a little too heavy to move around as well.

My rottweiler-labrador-german shepherd dog in the re-built tractor.

When I had moved the tractor inside I eventually re-designed it. It worked as it was, but I felt better when I added a wire-pen on the roof and made a way up for the rabbit so he could sit there and see more things than people's feet walking by. I also made doors to the side so I can open it and reach properly when cleaning. I did feel a bit bad about the cage in the start, as it was in a dark forgotten corner of the barn and I felt like I just put the rabbit in storage in it. It's also my smallest cage. But the second level and new doors made it more interesting for the rabbit, the way up is a nice reason for exercise and from the roof he gets a nice view around him. He can also say hello to my horse that's in the stall behind the cage, and I had noted that my horse tries to feed the rabbit hay. Or so it would seem from all hay that gets sprinkled over the cage.

Breeding

It's not unusual that I hear people express worry about keeping does together during kindling and pregnancies. They're worried that the does may kill each other's kits or in other ways harm the offspring.

These concerns are of course valid, but my experience is that does don't harm the young. Neither do bucks as a general rule. There are situations when a doe might be aggressive to kits but that is usually when kits from another doe's territory enters their own and if space is an issue. I know of caged does that hurt kits that came into her cage. In a colony however I expect that the does are going along well before you breed and then the kits will be considered family until they mature. I have yet to see any does hurt any kit in my colony, even in cases when they have been grumpy towards each other.

We have the responsibility to keep the rabbits in a good group where they can live together and raise their young without feeling stress or attacking the kits.

A risk with colony breeding is that the less dominant doe simply won't get pregnant. If they consider food or space to be scarce, the less dominant doe may absorb her kits before birth, so that the dominant does kits get a better chance of survival. This can be helped by providing fresh, rich feed as grass or garden scraps and to make sure they have enough space and distractions to not be in each other's faces all the time. I've mostly had trouble with this in winter when reproduction is already a bit stumped.

Introductions and Re-Introducing a Kit

I sometimes see a question about reintroducing kits with their mothers in a colony. I had a reason to try that recently, as I had changed my mind on whether I should keep a kit of the last litter or not. I decided I wanted one of the does. I simply put her back in with the other two does and it was a heartwarming moment when they both started grooming her immediately. She had been gone for a little over a month but there is no question that they remembered her.

Then they both started chasing her around, it was as if they wanted to tell her that just because she had been away from home there was no reason for her to think she had become something! It made me chuckle a bit. But it all calmed down pretty soon and now they act as if they never were apart.

That has not always been the case. I also tried to introduce Spira, my checkered giant doe, into the colony. I had her in a small cage inside it at first for a good couple of weeks, but the both sisters refused to accept her. I also tried to let her out at times but they charged her and chased her to no end. Even though I wanted to let them settle the pecking order and all, it was simply not fair to the young doe and I decided to pair her up with the 10 week old kit that I had also kept back.

I ended up dividing the colony into two sections, where the sisters, Kummin and Kyndel, and their newly re-introduced kit Dill had one section and Spira and Kyndel's daughter Sotöra shared the other section. It has worked very well and they all have company. In a way it's funny how the colony now is like I first planned it, with pairs instead of groups and three sections (if you count the bucks cage as one) for my breeders. But it turned out better than I could have imagined back then, and has expanded ridiculously fast.

I'm not sure I will keep both sisters. I think I'd rather have pairs than groups of uneven numbers. Some research has shown that rabbits in groups of two, four or six have less fights or dominance behavior than groups of three or five rabbits. I assume that with a large enough group it wouldn't matter, but I'm afraid that with three of them one will easily be bullied. Time will tell.

Keeping rabbits friendly

Sometimes people that are new to colonies express a concern about catching the kits and having them friendly.

My experience is that the kits attitude to people will mirror the does approach to us. Even raised in the colony, Kyndel's kits will be more skittish than Kummin's. Therefore I work to get the does friendly. By simply feeding them and not leaving until they have come forward to eat, I make them used to me. Eventually I try to pet them while they eat and when I can do that I consider them friendly enough. At that point it will be easy to pick them up and their kits will shoot forward to get fed as well. Sometimes I give them treats to enforce how much of a nice person I am and that it's good to come and say hi to me. Kummin's kits are wonderful in that manner. They will sniff at my hands, climb on my shoes and generally be pretty bothersome, especially when I'm cleaning their pen. But it's all very sweet as well.

I've met a few rabbits I couldn't get friendly enough, despite giving them treats and spending time in the pen with them. I simply won't breed those rabbits if they're does, and I'll try to replace them if they're bucks.

Building a new outdoor pen

Another thing I've worked on is a new pen. It's about the same size as the two grow-out pens I have outside and placed on the back of them. I intend to keep young does there and let the bucks share my first pens. I might add two openings with doors so I can open the both pens as one. I would need at least two such openings or else one rabbit may guard the opening and keep the others away. With two or more openings they won't get locked up or kept from food and water. I also want to be able to seal the openings in case I need to divide the pens again. I'm thinking of making tunnels and simply block them with a rock if necessary.

But to the construction of my new pen, I took pictures during the work as to give you all some insight in how I think and build. It's all built with scrap materials with an exception of the net. Since I'm using the back of my first pens as a wall, and they're not perfectly straight, I didn't care too much about making the new construction with perfect 90° angles either. Most of it is cut and nailed down at the spot.

I started with choosing where to build, and marked the area to get an idea of the size. I decided that I wanted the stump in the colony, to make for a nice shelf.

Next thing was to build the main frame. That was the hard part as I want it sturdy and all. As you can see already - it won't be straight. I realized that my outdoor rabbitry will look like a shabby town, but I like that look in a way, so I kept going.

I made a door and added boards to hold up the roof. I intended to keep part of it open and part of it covered, so that they got both protection from the rain and the option of sunlight on nice days.

With this done I buried the net. I dug out one section at a time and covered it with soil again. Make sure to secure the net properly and not leave any way in or out. I nailed it into the tree stump and covered with rocks to give the rabbits a way up. I also covered the sides with net but let the roof be at the time so I could easily move the boards that I wanted to make a floor with inside.

Since I later decided to make a proper floor instead of a dirt floor, I could have skipped this a step. But I didn't have that planned out to start with.

In Sweden, there is a law that winter hutches should have a raised floor. In a pen that can be made by simply making a floor and setting it onto bricks to leave air between the ground and the floor. It's a good idea to keep the rabbits dry in rainy weather and such, so they won't have to hop around in mud. However they don't need to have it all covered, so I just made a part of it into a floor. I need to remember that I can only keep a limited amount of rabbits in there as they all have to have access to the floor, the rest of the pen doesn't count in the winter when I calculate how much area each rabbit has.

I then added a board in the front to keep them from hiding under the floor, made some walls by stacking blocks and added a second floor as a self. Rabbits love shelves. If I keep any grow outs in the winter I'll make a more wind-tight and secure front to give them more protected space.

For the roof I used what I had at home.

Does and kits trying the pen

The rabbits enjoy their pen. I ended up with a bunch of bucks in there as I have nearly no does in my litters this year.

They are all really enjoyed the tree stump, as I had hoped. There's room for them to spread out and have their own space.

It's a nice way to relax, taking a cup of coffee out with me and just watching them.

Then I realized that dirt floors are hard to sanitize so I made a wood floor. Wood can be burnt and cleaned with disinfectants, or in the case of coccidia, with natrium hydroxide. Warm water with a good amount of natrium hydroxide will dissolve coccidia oocysts and most other parasites, virus and bacteria. Rinse well and make sure not to get any solution on your hands as it will burn.

In the two grow-out pens I laid a wood floor, quite simple and boring. In this pen however, since it had such an unusual shape with the tree stump and all, I made part of it a wooden floor, part of it bricks and part of it stones. I then used concrete to bind the bricks and stones together, and make a wash-able floor.

Above is a picture before the concrete was used, below is one with the concrete. Since I mixed and poured it a bit too late in the season, it wasn't quite dry yet when I took the picture.

Conclusion

Hey! Boyd here again. I find all of these pictures and ideas inspiring. This is more like my mind sees wild rabbits living than the way I have mine. The idea of them having more room to move about, me having room to walk inside and stand upright while interacting with my breeders appeals to me. The ability for them to socialize and even to create their own social structure appeals to me.

I feel that I would like to continue growing out my feeders after weaning (that are purposed as meat) in the mobile grazers like I have been doing. They get some of the benefits of living more naturally, on the ground and "finding" their own food. I get the benefit of anonymity. Personally, I find it easier on me to have a bunch of rabbits that all look alike and are nameless to me when it comes butchering day. I'll be honest about that. I DO NOT like the killing part, but am wise enough to understand that that's how nature works. Until that fateful day arrives, I want healthy, happy animals.

I think that since I don't have a barn, or presently live where I can have a barn that I'll have to do a hybrid colony that takes ideas from Megan's colony hutch and as many of Zab's features as possible and weld them all up together somehow. I have a 9'x 30' L shaped place on the north side of my house where my hutches are now. I should be able to

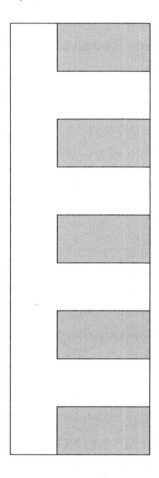

fence the whole area in and place 5 colony hutches that are entirely open on the bottom floor except for a ramp going up inside to the 2nd and 3rd floors of each. The 5 gray areas are the colony hutches (3'x 6' each) and the white areas are 3' walkways. The first level is 30" tall so that they can run, jump or even stand fully up everywhere in the 270 square feet with direct contact with the ground. The 2nd level will be 18" tall, insulated well and will be where the feed and water stations are in hopes that when the rabbits gather there they'll keep it warm enough that their water won't freeze in the winter. That will make the floor of the 3rd level 48" off the ground for easy access for cleaning. The 3rd floor will be a standard wire floor with trays underneath to catch any waste, and will have wire walls on 3 sides providing the availability of open air and long views. I expect it will be used the least. We'll see.

The additional square footage provided by the 2nd and 3rd floors of the colony hutches adds up to another 180 square feet. That makes a total of 450 square feet available to me to house my rabbits! You know what? Maybe I won't need the moveable grazers for feeders with that much space. I might be able to grow out the little bucks in one of the colony hutches and the little does in another until they're ready! We'll see.

I'll post pictures and updates about my project on The Urban Rabbit Project and in Zab's group Rabbits in Colonies in the spring of 2014.

We hope that this has given you some ideas too. Stop by and see us. Be sure to share pictures and tell stories about your experiences in either group as well!

This has been Volume 3 of The Urban Rabbit series. Don't miss any of the other Volumes.

Volume 2: Beyond The Pellet – Feeding Rabbits Naturally
http://www.amazon.com/dp/B00FZF1FCW

Volume 1: Backyard Meat Rabbits
http://www.amazon.com/dp/B00AG3X24M

Made in the USA
Las Vegas, NV
12 February 2022

43795494R00049